D0513846

chool

13633

e the

OWN...

THRILLERS

PIE CORBETT

**ILLUSTRATED BY
PETER BAILEY**

Belitha Press

To Teddy – reader
and writer of thrillers

HAMPSHIRE COUNTY LIBRARY	
1824157	
Peters	08-Aug-02
808	£7.99
184138254X	

First published in Great Britain in 2001 by

Belitha Press Limited, London House
Great Eastern Wharf
Parkgate Road, London SW11 4NQ

Copyright © Belitha Press Limited 2001
Text copyright © Pie Corbett 2001

Series editor: Mary-Jane Wilkins
Editors: Vic Parker, Russell Mclean
Designer: Sarah Goodwin
Illustrator: Peter Bailey

All rights reserved. No part of this book may be
reproduced or utilized in any form or by any means,
electronic or mechanical, including photocopying,
recording or by any information storage and retrieval
system, without permission in writing from the
publisher, except by a reviewer who may quote
brief passages in a review.

ISBN 1 84138 254 X

British Library Cataloguing in Publication Data for
this book is available from the British Library.

Printed by Omnia Books Ltd, Glasgow

10 9 8 7 6 5 4 3 2 1

CONTENTS

FEEL THE THRILL
THINKING ABOUT THRILLERS

It was quite dark now. Jo plodded down Weston Road, the bright street lights casting puddles of orange on the pavement. But she stopped at number 32 and stared. Somebody was coming down the steps. Yet hadn't her Mum told her that the house would be empty for another month? Jo pressed herself back, tight against the hedge. She felt safe in the dark.

It wasn't one person – there were two of them. They were carrying a heavy bundle that looked like a rolled-up carpet. One of them opened the back doors of a van. They began shoving the bundle in.

Of course, thought Jo, they must be removing some furniture. She was just about to come out from her hiding place, when one of them spoke.

"She's heavy!"

Jo froze.

Exciting stuff, isn't it? It makes you want to read on. Who are the people carrying the rolled-up carpet?

Is there really a girl inside? And if there is, is she alive? If you like reading exciting stories, then how about writing one too? This book will help you write your own thrilling adventure.

WHAT IS A THRILLER?

A thriller is a story that gives you plenty of frightening thrills and spills. It grips you from the word go and keeps you on the edge of your seat.

A thriller can be:
☆ an adventure story;
☆ a detective story;
☆ a kidnap story;
☆ a robbery story;
☆ an escape story;
☆ a chase story.

There might be:
☆ crooks, gangsters, robbers, villains, pirates, evil inventors, nasty teachers, mysterious strangers;
☆ police, detectives, a helpful professor, clever animals, loyal friends, brave kids, friendly grown-ups;
☆ 'goodies' who turn out to be bad;
☆ 'baddies' who turn out to be good.

WHAT DO I NEED TO WRITE MY OWN THRILLER?

The good thing about being a writer is that you don't need much equipment – just some paper or a notebook, a pen, and a place to write.

You can write almost anywhere. Many writers set up in the corner of a room. Michael Morpurgo writes lying on his bed!

Some writers write straight on to a computer. Remember always to save your work as you write.

A good dictionary (or computer spell check) is helpful. A thesaurus is also useful for looking up alternatives to words you use a lot.

WRITING TIP

Some of the writing terms in this book are explained in the glossary on page 62. On pages 58–60 there are also checklists to help with spelling, punctuation and making new paragraphs.

READ ... READ ... AND READ SOME MORE

If you want to become good at writing thrillers then you have to read plenty. The more you read, the more ideas you will have about how to write your own. When you are reading:

☆ notice how stories are structured;
☆ notice which incidents sound exciting;
☆ think about how the writer keeps the pace going;
☆ think about how the paragraphs and sentences are written.

All new writers begin by imitating good writers.
Here's a list of some of the best writers of thrillers.

Enid Blyton
Theresa Breslin
Gillian Cross
Susan Gates
Anthony Horowitz
Pete Johnson
Gary Paulsen
Philip Pullman
Jeremy Strong
Robert Swindells

WRITING TIP

Always have a book by your bed and read every night.

TRAPPING IDEAS

Writers are like thieving magpies. They are always on the lookout for ideas, from all sorts of places.

☆ **Listen to what people say**

You may overhear snippets of talk that would make good dialogue: "...and then I saw she'd stolen it..."

☆ **Watch people**

Spotting interesting people may give you ideas for characters: an old man hobbling along, carrying a pair of new shoes, two boys climbing over a fence and sprinting away.

☆ Be curious

Wonder about everyday things. For instance, why does the woman at number 17 spend so much time looking through her curtains?

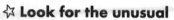

☆ Look for the unusual

Here are three odd things I saw that sparked ideas.

1 A black cat with a goldfish in its mouth walking along the street.

2 An old woman with a football in a plastic bag.

3 A llama crossing a railway line.

☆ Notice places that look scary

For instance, a deserted railway station with a waiting room door that bangs to and fro in the wind is just the sort of place where somebody might hide in a thrilling story.

KEEP A WRITING JOURNAL

When you have an idea, write it down. Otherwise, you may forget it! Most writers keep a journal in which they jot ideas. Make your own out of a jotter or exercise book – a blank notebook with a hard cover is ideal.

TIME TO WRITE

1 Start off your writing journal with a list of your favourite authors and thrillers. Jot down why you like these authors and books.

2 Now start collecting some ideas. Jot down:
★ a few possible names for characters;
★ two or three places that have atmosphere;
★ strange or frightening things that have happened to you and your friends;
★ odd people and things you have seen;
★ interesting sayings that people use.

3 Use your writing journal as a place to jot down anything you might be able to use in your stories. Always be on the lookout for good ideas!

WRITERS AT WORK

STARTING YOUR OWN STORY

All writers have five 'servants' to help them when they sit down to write: who? where? when? what? and how?

1 Who?

Think about your characters. Thrillers always have at least one main goodie and baddie. Also decide if you want to write the story as if you were the main character, for example: *I turned to run but my way was blocked*, or as if you are writing about someone else, for example: *Tom turned to run but his way was blocked.*

2 Where?

The next big decision is where to set the story. If you use places you know well, you can think of details to describe the setting and make it seem real. Alan Garner placed the action in *The Weirdstone of Brisingamen* on the hills where he lives.

3 When?

Most stories are set in the past. This makes it sound as if the story has already happened, for example: *I strolled down the hill and waited at the bus stop.*

Some stories are written in the present tense, as if the story is happening as you read. For example: *I stroll down the hill and wait at the bus stop.* This can make it more exciting – but you have to remember to stay in the present tense and not slip back into the past.

4 What?

You need some ideas about what might happen in your story. This is called a plot outline, such as: A teacher tries to hypnotise the class into carrying out robberies.

5 How?

You also need a trigger. This is an event that sets the story going. For example: the main character, Jo, is late for school and the teacher makes her stay in at playtime. The teacher then tries to hypnotise her.

Let's think a bit more about some of these five servants.

GET UNDER THE CHARACTER'S SKIN

Although your thriller will have more than one person in it, you need to decide who will be the focus of your story – your main character. Don't forget that your reader must like your main character, or they will not want to read about him or her.

You can have more than one main character – but don't have too many or it will be difficult to make them all sound real.

Before writing, think about:

1 The characters' names
For example: Jo Stannard, Tom Huxford; Bodger O'Neill, Lanky Lane; Dizzy Davies.

oh rats!

2 Special details
Choose one or two details about each main character, such as the following.
☆ Something they wear, such as a pair of red leggings and parrot earrings.
☆ Something about how they look, such as a woman whose eyes are jet black and stare in a frightening way.
☆ How your characters walk, such as a stranger who walks with long strides and a bent back.
☆ A favourite expression they use, such as, *"Oh rats!"* or *"It's a load of malarkey."*

3 Character type

Now decide what sort of person each character is: aggressive, happy-go-lucky, friendly, keen to lead, spiteful, unkind, brainy, bold, a misery guts, angry, etc. It can be fun to select contrasting characters, so if one is bossy then the other could be shy.

When you are writing, keep thinking about your character types and what that sort of person would say or do next.

WRITING TIP

Why not try writing different stories about the same character or characters?

SET THE SCENE

You need to decide where to start the story and to imagine different settings to use during the story.

To create a comfortable atmosphere, you could put your characters in the kitchen, by a warm fire, in a classroom, in a park or in a library, for example.

Move the characters into scary places if you want your readers to feel afraid. To create a frightening atmosphere, you could put your characters in a deserted house, a wood, at the top of a tower, in a dark alleyway, on a stairwell in a block of flats, on a lonely moor.

Describing the weather, time of day and time of year can also make your story more thrilling. For example, a storm or a dark night are more scary than a hot sunny afternoon.

> ### WRITING TIP
> Do not write about your settings in too much detail – just write enough to give your readers a picture in their mind.

PLAN THE PLOT

All stories need a plot outline. This can be quite simple. Here are some examples.

☆ **Getting lost**

Two children get lost in a wood or in the town. They find, or overhear, something that leads them into danger.

☆ **Trapped**

The main characters get trapped in an old house where a gang of spies is planning to kill the Prime Minister.

✰ Kidnapped
A new girl at school is kidnapped and the main characters find a clue to where she is held prisoner.

✰ Mad inventor
A friendly inventor creates a way of turning mud into gold. The formula disappears.

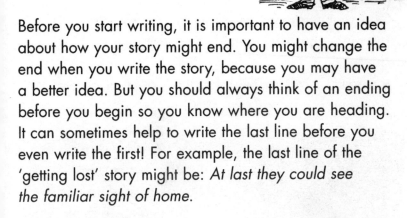

✰ Something is stolen
A local bank is robbed and the main character finds the robbers' hiding place.

Before you start writing, it is important to have an idea about how your story might end. You might change the end when you write the story, because you may have a better idea. But you should always think of an ending before you begin so you know where you are heading. It can sometimes help to write the last line before you even write the first! For example, the last line of the 'getting lost' story might be: *At last they could see the familiar sight of home.*

PULL THE TRIGGER
The trigger is a small event that sets the plot of your story going. It is useful to have the main characters doing something fairly ordinary in the first couple of paragraphs and then make something happen just to start the tale running.

Here are some ideas for triggers.

☆ A hobby
Two children go fishing. One of them falls in the lake.
Who will come to the rescue?

☆ Noises
Odd sounds are coming from the professor's workshop.
The main characters decide to investigate.

☆ The box
A parcel arrives marked 'Fragile – open with care'.
Someone clumsy tries to open it!

☆ Night lights
Two friends see strange
lights at night. They
decide to stay up one
night and solve the mystery.

WRITING TIP

Don't waste time thinking of a title before
you begin writing. Most writers use a
working title. Choose this without much fuss, just to start
off. You can change it later if you think of a better idea.

SHAPING UP

Think about the shape of your plot before you start to write. The simplest structure for a story is to begin with everything being all right. Then a series of events happen that lead the characters into a dilemma or problem, a mystery or something that needs sorting out. The rest of the story is a series of events that solve the problem, so that at the end everything is all right again. This plot shape can be shown rather like a hill.

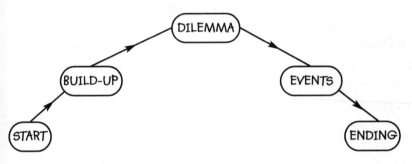

Other stories have the dilemma right at the beginning, so the story is about how the problem is solved. The shape of this type of plot is rather like going down hill.

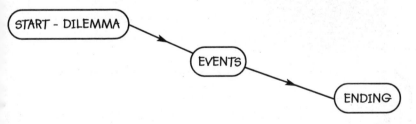

Thrillers often have cliffhangers – exciting events that lead your characters to the brink of disaster. The shape of this type of plot can be like a series of hills (see next page).

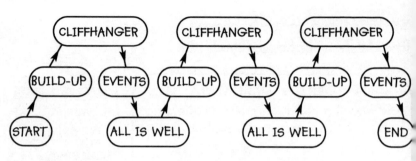

To organize your plot, decide which shape you would like to use and write it out in your writer's journal. Then, underneath each part of the shape, jot down what will happen in your story. You could start with the basic plot shape, like this:

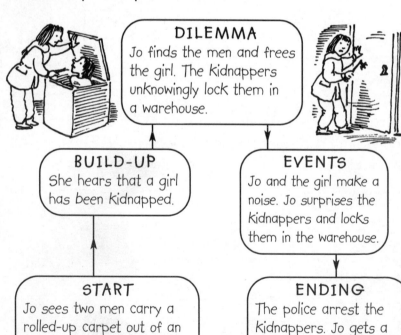

DILEMMA
Jo finds the men and frees the girl. The kidnappers unknowingly lock them in a warehouse.

BUILD-UP
She hears that a girl has been kidnapped.

EVENTS
Jo and the girl make a noise. Jo surprises the kidnappers and locks them in the warehouse.

START
Jo sees two men carry a rolled-up carpet out of an empty house. She suspects there is a girl inside.

ENDING
The police arrest the kidnappers. Jo gets a reward. Jo and the girl become best friends.

You might then decide to change your plot
to a different shape, like this:

START – DILEMMA
Jo is trying to get into a warehouse.
Earlier, she had seen two suspicious-looking
men – were they kidnapping someone?
She had overheard them say they were
going to the warehouse.

EVENTS
Jo finds a way in, discovers a kidnapped
girl and frees her. They hear the
kidnappers coming and hide in the
warehouse. The kidnappers unknowingly
lock them inside. The girls make a noise,
so the crooks investigate. Jo locks them
in the warehouse instead!

ENDING
The girls call the police, who arrest
the kidnappers. The girl tells Jo she
overheard the crooks talking about
another gang, who are planning a
diamond robbery. The girls decide
to set up a detective agency together.
Their first mission is to foil the
diamond robbery...

Or you might want to try a third plot shape, perhaps like this:

CLIFFHANGER
Jo starts to open the crate, but the kidnappers return. She hides.

CLIFFHANGER
The crooks search for the girls.

BUILD-UP
Jo cycles to a warehouse she heard the men talk about. A girl is crying inside a locked crate.

EVENTS
The crooks take the girl away in a truck. Jo jumps into the back.

BUILD-UP
The girls hear the truck coming back. They hide.

START
Jo suspects that two men are kidnapping someone.

ALL IS WELL
The kidnappers tie up the girl in a barn and drive away. Jo frees her.

CLIFFHANGER
The girls run away, chased by the man – right into the path of a speeding car!

EVENTS
The girls jump into the crooks' truck and speed away.

BUILD-UP
The man who serves them seems strange. The girls overhear him on the phone: "They're here." He is one of the crooks' gang!

EVENTS
The car just misses them. It's the police! The girls blurt out their story.

ALL IS WELL
The girls stop at a service station for food and drink.

ENDING
The crooks arrive and are arrested. The girls decide to start their own detective agency.

You could make your plot either simpler or more detailed, as you like. Remember that some parts of your plot could end up as more than one paragraph of writing. Also, as you write the story, you may find other ideas creeping in. The story planner will give you a start and a direction for your story, but be prepared to change direction if you have good ideas in the course of writing.

TIME TO WRITE

1 In your writing journal, make notes about the following:

Who? Jot down some possible names for your main character, some ideas for special details about them and what type of person they might be.

Where? Write down some ideas for settings.

When? Make notes about what time of day your story might start. What is the weather like? Will you write your story in the present or the past?

What? Jot down some basic plot outlines to choose from.

How? Write ideas for triggers to get your story going.

2 Draw a story planner and decide on the shape that you want your story to take.

TRICKS OF THE TRADE
HOW TO HYPNOTISE YOUR READER

All the best writers do a lot of thinking before they start to write their stories. Once you have your characters, setting and plot outline, you need to think about the words and sentences you will use to tell your story. This chapter tells you about a few tricks of the trade that thriller writers use to make their stories really exciting.

MAKE YOUR CHARACTERS SEEM REAL
1 Describing your characters
To make your characters seem real, you need to describe their appearance. You don't need too much detail. For instance, if you describe a character as having a cruel mouth, you may not need to say more. After all, your readers will have met nasty people before and will therefore imagine their own picture of the character.

Here are some ideas for describing
your characters.

☆ **How they talk**

For example, *a sharp, harsh
voice* suggests an unpleasant
person; *a rich laugh* suggests
a kind person.

☆ **How they walk**

For example, *He strode into the room*
suggests someone in charge.

☆ **What their features are like**

For example, someone might have *slim, delicate
fingers that could unpick a lock*; *a thin smile* might
imply that a character is mean; *his eyes gleamed*
could suggest that he is greedy, whereas *his eyes
glittered* hints that he is crazy.

☆ **What their
clothes are like**

For example, *a sleek black
suit* suggests a character is
precise; a girl who wears
*faded jeans with flowery
patches* sounds as if she is
easy-going and optimistic.

2 Describing what your characters do

When you are writing, keep thinking about what your
characters might do in certain situations. Think about
your character's type. Ask yourself: What would this
character be feeling now? What would they do?

Imagine you have a bossy character called Amy and a shy character called Hal. They meet a gang of bullies. What will they do?

☆ Amy might tell Hal what to do: *"Quick,"* yelled Amy, *"Run for it!" Hal followed Amy as she sped for the trees.*

☆ Amy might decide to stand up to the bullies: *"This is a free country,"* snapped Amy. She put her hands on her hips and glared at the gang leader.

☆ On the other hand, Hal is more likely to run: *Without waiting to see what was going to happen, Hal ran for cover, leaving Amy behind.*

☆ Or he might agree to do what the bullies want: *"OK,"* said Hal, shaking his head. *"Here's all my money – just leave us alone."*

WRITING TIP

You may find that as you write, your characters decide to do things that you had not planned – don't worry if the characters seem to take over!

3 Making your characters talk

Think about what your characters might say in a certain situation. Different characters would say different things. For instance, imagine that a character meets an old friend. What might they say?

☆ An angry character might say:
   "What on earth are you doing hanging around here?"
☆ A happy character might say:
   "Hey, great to see you."

Use adverbs to tell your readers how a character speaks. A character might speak slowly or carefully, quietly, loudly, cautiously, savagely, angrily, cruelly, fearlessly, bravely, firmly and so on. You might also want to use a speech verb now and then. For example: he muttered or mumbled, whispered, moaned, groaned, hissed, spat, snarled, growled, yawned, bellowed, roared, snapped. But be careful not to use adverbs and speech verbs all the time, or they lose their power and just become tiresome to read.

Some stories are spoiled because the writer uses too much speech and it becomes a long list. Soon the reader forgets who is speaking. It can also be hard to know what is happening. For example:

   "Hi there Dave."
   "Good to see you."
   "Shall we go to the Centre?"

26

"OK, if you want."
"Yes, it would be fun."
"I like the shops."
"So do I."

You can avoid this problem by having only three or four exchanges of speech at a time.

WRITING TIP

Listen carefully to how people speak and make your dialogue seem real by using everyday expressions. Think about the kind of words a character is likely to use. For instance, an old professor might use some long, complicated words. Three friends might have a favourite saying that they use a lot.

MIX A BREW OF THRILLING INGREDIENTS

In thrillers certain scenes always make the reader feel nervous. Here are some ideas.

☆ **Footsteps**

Introduce the sound of footsteps walking or running, but don't say whose they are. This will make your readers feel uneasy.

☆ **Dark alleyways**

Taking the main characters down a dark lane is always a good recipe for frightening your readers.

☆ **Deserted houses**

Deserted houses have been used in thrilling stories and films for years.

A deserted house could be a hiding place for robbers, treasure or a kidnap victim.

☆ **Dodgy-looking people**

Unusual people are excellent ingredients for a thriller. They might be strangers to the area. Or simply characters who behave in a suspicious way or who look shifty – for instance, someone with a hat pulled down as if to disguise himself.

☆ **The glint of the sun on metal**

This suggests a gun or a knife. It can be used to scare the reader into thinking that something awful is about to happen. Of course, it might turn out that it was just the sun shining on a bicycle!

KERPOW! WRITE ACTION PARAGRAPHS

In thrillers, there are always paragraphs that have plenty of action, such as a chase, a fight, an argument, or a scene in which someone is captured.

These exciting events can be difficult to write about, even if the writer can see what is happening clearly in their mind. For example: *Kerpow! Jason kicked out. Bang! Splat! That sorted the baddies out.* This language is fine for a comic book, but would be disappointing in a story without pictures.

There are a few simple rules to follow when you are writing thrilling action scenes.

☆ Imagine what is happening – but keep it short. A brief tussle is more dramatic than a long, drawn-out fight.
☆ Describe what you see in your imagination.
☆ Use a balance of short and long sentences.
☆ Use powerful verbs to describe the action.

Here's an example:

Without thinking, Tom dived forwards and grabbed the guard's knife arm. The knife clattered to the ground. Tom pinned the guard up against the cave wall. There was a yell from behind him and Tom felt himself being pulled backwards. Strong fingers were digging into his flesh. Tom dropped to one knee, lunged back with the metal bar. But it was too late. The room flooded with light. A harsh voice barked out a command...

WRITING TIP

Here are some action verbs: grip, grab, grasp, kick, lunge, poke, smack, crack, punch. Don't forget to describe sounds too, such as: clattered, bark, crack, snap, bang, explosion, roar, yell, scream.

WORD WATCHING

The man went down the road. This is a dull sentence.
It doesn't create a strong picture in the reader's mind.
But it could be improved quite easily.

☆ Try using powerful verbs:
  The man rushed down the road.
☆ Try using precise nouns:
  Tom went down the High Street.
☆ Try using carefully chosen
  adjectives and adverbs:
  *The slim man went cautiously
  down the road.*
☆ Try rearranging words: *Down the road went the man.*
☆ Try including some new information or detail: *The man,
  clutching a bulky package, went down the road.*

*The tired, weary, old, thin, small man went down the
road.* This sentence sounds odd because there are too
many adjectives. They clash against each other and
reduce the power of the words. So choose your
adjectives with care.

Sometimes you don't need one. For example: *The wet
water dripped on to the floor.* This sentence
sounds odd because you don't need to
tell the reader that the water is wet.
Also be careful not to use
adjectives that mean the same
sort of thing, for example:
*The tired, weary, sleepy
cat dozed.*

WRITING TIP
Only use an adjective when it tells the reader something new that they need to know.

STUNNING SPECIAL EFFECTS

All writers have a few techniques which can create different effects in their writing. Try using these special effects to make your writing more powerful.

1 Similes

A simile is a descriptive way of comparing one thing to another. Either use the word 'like': *The moon looked like a silver claw.* Or use the word 'as': *The moon was as thin as a claw.*

2 Metaphors

A metaphor is a bit like a simile. But in a simile, you say that one thing is *like* another. In a metaphor, you say that one thing *is* another. For example, this is a simile: *The moon was like a silver claw, reaching down to the dark pine trees.* This is a metaphor: *The silver claw of the moon reached down to the dark pine trees.*

Both similes and metaphors help to create powerful pictures.

3 Personification

Personification makes an object seem human. You either describe an object as if it looks human, for example: *The huge cave mouth gaped at him.* Or describe it as if it is doing something that a human might do, for example: *The shadows shook their heads.*

Personification makes objects seem alive. This can be very frightening.

4 Alliteration

Alliteration is the repetition of similar sounds. This can make a line atmospheric. In this example, the sound 'sh' is repeated: *The shadows shivered and shook their heads.*

5 Onomatopoiea

An onomatopoeia is a word that sounds like its meaning. In *The busy bees buzzed*, the repetition of the 'b', 's', and 'z' sounds help to create the buzzing sound of the bees.

6 Hooks

A hook is a hint that a writer drops into a story to suggest that something might be going to happen. For example: *As the detective burst through the door and scanned the room, he could see that whoever lived there had just left in a terrible hurry. The window was flung wide open.*

A radio was mumbling to itself in the kitchen. A half-drunk mug of coffee still steamed gently on the desk. Next to it lay an open book – an open book with a page ripped hastily out of it... Here, the hook is the missing page. The reader wonders who has it and what it says.

Hooks catch your readers' interest and keep them turning the pages. They can also move a plot along. For example: *The professor carefully examined the battered leather book. When he reached the place where the page had been ripped out, he frowned. "Yes, I can tell you what this page said," he sighed heavily. "And who might have taken it, too..."*

Hooks don't always have to be vital clues. Sometimes a writer might use a hook that turns out to be unimportant. This is called a red herring. It helps to keep readers guessing right to the end. So once you have decided how you want your story to finish, you can use hooks and red herrings to intrigue your readers.

JUST FOR STARTERS

Isn't this paragraph boring?
He went down the road. He went into the shop. He bought a loaf of bread. He came outside. He crossed the road. A car nearly hit him. He was frightened.

The sentences all begin in the same way! Make sure you vary the start of your sentences to keep your reader's attention. Here are some ways to do this:

☆ Start with an adverb: *Carefully, she opened the door.*

☆ Start with a word that ends in 'ing': *Panting, she paused at the bottom of the hill.*

☆ Start with a word that ends in 'ed': *Startled, she spun round.*

☆ Start with a connective: *Although I was tired, I ran as fast as I could.*

WRITING TIP

Try not to start sentences with 'and' or 'but' – particularly at the opening of a new paragraph. Some writers do this occasionally, when they want to create a particular effect for their readers. For example, a writer might close a story with the sentence: And so they made their way home. However, in most cases, beginning a sentence with 'and' or 'but' is thought to be bad grammar.

STYLISH SENTENCES

What do you think of this paragraph?

The key turned in the lock.
Jo stared. Tom gasped.
The key rasped. The door
creaked. It opened. The
children ran. They hid.
The man entered. They
shook. He searched.

Yes – too many short sentences sound odd.

Is this next paragraph any better?

The key turned in the lock and the door creaked.
Jo stared and Tom gasped. The key rasped but
the door opened. The children ran and they hid.
The man entered and he searched.

This time the writing sounds odd because
there are too many compound sentences.

What about this?

As the key turned in the lock,
Jo stared. Tom gasped while
the key rasped. Although the
door creaked, it opened. The
children ran so that they could
hide. As the man entered to
search the room, they shook.

The writing still sounds odd,
doesn't it? In this case, there are
too many complex sentences.

Finally, read this.

Jo stared. The key was turning slowly in the lock. Who was about to enter the room? Tom gasped! The key rasped and the door creaked open. Without thinking, the children ran to hide behind the sofa. As the man entered to search the room, they shook...

This time the writing is good because different types of sentence are used.

☆ Simple sentences are useful for drama and clarity, for example: *Jo stared.*

☆ Compound sentences are often easy to read. They also keep a story flowing smoothly along, for example: *The key rasped and the door creaked open.*

☆ Complex sentences can add extra layers of meaning, for example: *As the man entered to search the room, they shook.* Complex sentences help you to explain, justify, reason, argue, show what is happening elsewhere, or give alternative views.

☆ Questions help to draw the reader into the action, for example: *Who was about to enter the room?*

☆ Exclamations help to add emphasis and drama, for example: *Tom gasped!*

WRITING TIP

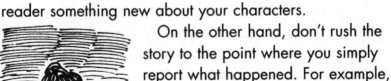

To help you write complex sentences, here is a list of some common connectives: after, although, as, as if, as long as, as though, because, before, if, in case, once, since, than, that, though, till, until, unless, when(ever), where(ever), whereas, while.

PACE YOURSELF

While you are writing, try to see what is happening in your mind. Concentrate on this and watch what happens.

But remember that you don't need to write down every detail. Too much description can slow down the pace of your story. So keep your plot going by just focusing on the key scenes. Miss out anything that isn't essential. For instance, you don't need to write about every meal your characters eat, or what they do when they're getting ready for bed – unless these scenes develop your plot or tell your reader something new about your characters.

On the other hand, don't rush the story to the point where you simply report what happened. For example, look at this dreadful ending: *The police arrived. The robbers got caught. The children went home.*

Try using connectives to help you miss out boring bits, while keeping

the pace moving. Flick through some stories
and jot down in your writer's journal
some typical paragraph openers, such
as: suddenly, in a flash, at that moment,
later that afternoon, in the morning,
without warning, after breakfast.

A SHORT STORY OR A LONG YARN?

Before you start writing, think about how long you want
your story to be. You don't have to decide on an exact
number of words or pages, but it's good to have an idea
of the overall length you're aiming for. For instance, do
you want to write a short story? Or a whole novel, with
chapters and illustrations? How much time do you have
for your writing? An hour? A day? A week or more?

Look at your plan and decide whether each part of your
story will be one paragraph, a couple of paragraphs or
a whole chapter. If you do this, you can make sure that
each section of your story is evenly balanced. Whether
your story is long or short, you want to avoid rushing
some bits of it and writing too much for others.

TIME TO WRITE

You are almost ready to start your story. First, make some more notes in your writer's journal. All top writers do a lot of thinking like this to help with their writing. Brainstorm some ideas and jot down whatever comes into your head for:

★ character description, action and dialogue;
★ frightening scenes;
★ action paragraphs;
★ powerful and precise words to use;
★ similes, metaphors and personification;
★ alliteration and onomatopoeia;
★ some exciting exclamations;
★ some useful questions to interest your reader;
★ some powerful sentences.

Use these later on if you get stuck when you're writing your story.

PUTTING PEN TO PAPER

KICK-START YOUR WRITING

Ready to write? Before you finally start, read this chapter. Each section will help you through a different stage of your story.

MAKING A FLYING START

Your opening sentence is very important. You need to grab your readers' interest, or they may not want to read on. Here are five ways to open your story.

1 Start with the name of your main character
For example: *Meg stared out of the window.* This introduces the main character straight away. It can also help to get the action going, for example: *Pete ran for his life.*

2 Use a spoken question
For example: *"Where on earth do you think you're going?"* or *"What is that shining in the gutter?"*

This raises a question in the reader's mind and helps to start off the action.

3 Use an exclamation

For example: *"Jump, just jump!"* or *"Quick, hide in here!"* This provides a surprise at the start of the story that will grab the reader's attention.

4 Use a dramatic event

For example: *The car screeched to a halt... The bomb exploded... The robbery began just after school had ended...* This plunges your readers straight into the story. Don't forget to use short sentences for impact.

5 Use the setting

The setting can create a tense atmosphere. For example: *Nobody in their right mind ever went down Fear Alley, for it was too dark even on the brightest day.*

FIRST PARAGRAPHS – ATTENTION-GRABBERS

Use your first paragraph to do several important jobs.

1 Introduce your main character

Show what your main character is like through the way they behave. For instance, if your main character is grumpy, you might begin like this: *Sam scowled at her mother. She turned on her heel and stormed out of the room.*

On the other hand, if you want your reader to know that Sam is a happy, easy-going sort of person, you might begin like this: *Sam grinned at her mother. She turned round and, with a wave, slipped out of the room.*

2 Hide your main character

If you hide your main character, you can use your first paragraph to set up an exciting mystery. For example: *She stared out of the window and wondered when on earth she would arrive. The towns sped by in a blur. The train rattled on. Far behind was her home, her school, her family. She gripped her bag and waited.*

This opening creates interest and suspense. The reader is left wondering who the girl is, where she is going, and why she has left home.

3 Set the scene

You don't have to make your main character the focus of your first paragraph at all – you can describe a setting instead. This can not only create a thrilling atmosphere, it can also introduce a place where a key event will occur later. For example: *On all sides, the trees towered high overhead. It was like being inside a cathedral.*

A dark cathedral. But it was not only the darkness, for there was also a stillness. Nothing moved, not even the slightest breath of wind. Although it was quite still there were noises. Not in the daytime, but at night.

This setting scares your readers straight away. But don't forget that you can always paint a comfortable scene in your first paragraph, then scare your readers with a nasty surprise a few paragraphs later.

THE SECOND PARAGRAPH – THE WIND-UP

In your second paragraph, you need to start the action moving. To get off to a simple start, you could think of something you do a lot and describe your characters doing that, for example, walking to the shops, cleaning the car, going fishing, and so on. Choose something you know well and add detail. For instance, if your characters are fishing, instead of writing: *He picked up his rod*, you could write: *He picked up his new telecaster rod.* The detail makes the action sound real.

Look back at the opening paragraph on page 42 about the girl on the train. This could be the second paragraph: *At long last, Elisa arrived at Blackstone Station. She swung her bag on to her shoulder and jumped down on to the platform. She pushed her way through the ticket barrier and wandered along the high street.*

The shops were empty. It was a quiet Saturday afternoon. Elisa strolled down the street towards the police station.

The second paragraph uses the ordinary experience of getting off a train and walking up a street. It also introduces a hook: why is Elisa making her way to the police station?

If you decide to use your first paragraph to set the scene, then you can use your second paragraph to introduce your main characters. Look at this story opening:

Caves were formed thousands of years ago. Who knows what caves could tell if only they had voices. Who hid inside Huntsman's Cave? Which tribe might have made it a home? What creatures had made it a lair? Only the bones left at the back of the cave could tell something of this story. Only the flint stone arrowhead, waiting to be found. Only the desperate message scrawled on the wall.

Harry and Leila stared into the cave. The torch light stabbed the darkness. They made their way carefully, crouching low so as not to bang their heads. The sides of the cave were damp and glistening. Some way ahead the torch light

*flickered across what looked like bones. The children
stopped in their tracks and stared.*

Here, the second paragraph both introduces the
main characters and gets the action going. Immediately,
it picks up on the bones mentioned in the first paragraph.
Whose bones? What has happened?

NAIL-BITERS

You need to create suspense to make your thriller really
exciting. One useful tactic is to make everything go well
for a paragraph or two, to lull your readers into a false
sense of security. Make sure that your characters seem
relaxed and happy.

For example, look at the following three paragraphs.
In the first, the writer introduces the main character.
In the second paragraph, the writer shows the main
character doing something ordinary. In the third
paragraph, things are still going well.

*"And close the door behind you," snapped Miss Jarvis.
Chris pulled the door to, leant against it and breathed
a sigh of relief. At last she was out of detention. That
would be the last time that she would answer back
to Miss Jarvis, she thought. It just wasn't worth it.*

Chris ran out of school, down to the bus stop. Ali was still there, so she knew that he had stayed behind just for her. She grinned at him. Without saying a word they waited, shuffling their feet to keep out the cold.

It wasn't long before a number 61 trundled into sight. Chris and Ali flashed their bus passes at the driver and made their way to the back of the bus. This was their domain. They settled down as the bus lurched up the street towards Kingstown centre. They saw the same old sights out of the window – the chippie, Mrs Hesketh's cake shop, the back of Woolies, then the fields. As the bus rattled along, the two friends laughed and joked. They planned what they would do at the weekend.

By the end of the third paragraph, the writer has created a cosy, comfortable atmosphere. Two friends are enjoying a chat, settled down on the familiar bus route home.

Once your readers are thinking that everything is going well, it's time to introduce a nasty surprise to create suspense. Your characters might hear something suspicious, for example: footsteps, a twig snapping, a scratching noise.

Or they might see something odd, such as an eye, a hand, or a shadow moving. Your reader will feel as if something frightening is about to happen.

When you are writing a suspense paragraph there are a number of tactics you can use.

☆ Use short sentences to create dramatic tension and balance these with some longer ones that add detail.
☆ Don't reveal what makes the noise or what is seen – keep your readers guessing.
☆ Make your main character ask a question, wondering what is making the noise, or what it is that they've just glimpsed.
☆ Use some frightening description, such as mentioning the darkness or the cold.
☆ Describe the reactions of your characters.

Read this paragraph and notice how the writer has created suspense:

The bus ground to a halt. Chris stared out of the window. They were in a stretch of countryside she did not recognize. The bus driver was no longer at the wheel. The engine had stopped. There was no-one else on board and the two friends looked at each other. From outside the bus came a sound

– a scraping noise.
A scratching sound.
Like nails scratching metal.
Like claws. Ali peered through
the misty windows. "What's
that?" he asked, pointing at a shadow.
"I don't know," muttered Chris...

WRITING TIP

Collect some suspense paragraph starters in your writer's journal, such as: suddenly... quickly... without warning... silently... in terror... in horror... a scream broke the silence...

WRITING CLIFFHANGERS

Cliffhangers are events that keep readers on the edge of their seat by putting the main character close to disaster.

Harry moved forward towards the pile of bones. He could just make out the outline of what he thought was a skull. He shuddered. At that moment the torch beam flickered and went out. Leila gave a short scream from behind him. Then there was silence. Harry took one more pace forward but where he expected to feel the floor of the cave, he felt nothing.

It was as though he had stepped off the edge of the world. He was falling, falling — falling to his death for all he knew.

Most thriller novels use a cliffhanger at the end of each chapter, so that the reader is desperate to read on. This is why people sometimes say that a book was so exciting they couldn't put it down. No sooner has the character escaped from one perilous situation than there is a build-up into another.

You could try using the following situations as cliffhangers: being captured by a gang, falling off a cliff, being chased by a shark, having ten seconds until a bomb explodes.

WRITING TIP

Don't worry if your story isn't long enough to be split up into chapters, you can still use cliffhangers to grip your readers. Write your main character into a possibly disastrous position at the end of a paragraph, so your readers have to read on to the next paragraph to find out what happens.

TYING UP YOUR TALE

It can be quite difficult to think of an ending to your story, especially if you did not think about this right at the beginning. It is no good just writing *I woke up and it was all a dream*. This will leave your readers feeling cheated!

Thrillers often have a surprise ending – such as when you discover that someone you thought was a goodie turns out to have been helping the enemy all along! One author who is very clever at writing endings the reader does not see coming is Paul Jennings.

Here are some other ideas for ways to end your thriller.

1 Tie up your story neatly
A simple but very satisfying way to end your story is to make sure that the villains get their comeuppance and the main characters win the day.

2 Go back to the beginning
Look back to the first paragraph. Can you use the beginning to create a contrast with your ending? For instance, maybe your main character has changed — if he was feeling angry at the start of the story, perhaps he is now feeling calmer.

Sometimes it helps to create a contrast if you reuse some of the opening sentence. For instance, if your opening paragraph is: *The lane was quite deserted. Deserted, except for the girl. She was sobbing quietly into a large, red handkerchief.* Your end paragraph could be: *Ros pulled out her red handkerchief.*

She turned to Tim and laughed. "Well, this will never harm us again," she said, as she threw it on the fire.

3 Take your characters home

Once all the mysteries in your thriller are solved and the story is over, it can help to add on a final paragraph in which the main characters make their way home. This leads your readers gently out of the tale and leaves them feeling satisfied.

4 Leave your story on a question

Finishing your story on a question suggests that there might be another story (a sequel) and leaves your readers wondering. Sometimes, the writer directly addresses the reader, as in this example.

Ros pulled out the red handkerchief. She turned to Tim and laughed. "Well, this will never harm us again," she said, as she threw it on the fire. The flames flickered and soon the handkerchief disappeared. The two children turned for home. Surely now they would be happy... You've read their tale, what do you think?

5 Leave one loose thread

Ending a thriller by leaving one loose thread is a cunning trick that continues the suspense of the story. The main characters think that everything is sorted out and that all is well. But there is one thing they forget about or overlook – one loose end that only the reader notices has been left undone.

Ros pulled out the red handkerchief. She turned to Tim and laughed. "Well, I won't be needing that any more," she said, as she threw it on the fire. The flames flickered and soon the handkerchief disappeared. The two children turned for home. As they made their way over the hill, they didn't see a red blur caught in the bushes. A closer look would have shown a fragment of red handkerchief...

6 Reflecting on the story

Once the tale has been wrapped up, it can help to add on an extra paragraph in which there is some thinking about what has happened and what it means. You can do this in different ways.

☆ Some stories end with the main characters being confronted by an adult. The adult then comments on what has happened. For example:

Mrs Swabey stared at the two children. Annabel looked down at her trainers, Mel gulped. They knew that they were in trouble. "I've told you a thousand times not to play near the dump. Well, that's it – you're not going out at all next week. Playing detectives! Whatever next?"

☆ The main characters themselves might reflect. For example:

Mel turned to Annabel. "Do you think he'll be all right?"

"I hope so," replied her sister. "He still has the golden arrow – and besides, he's the only one who knows where the treasure was buried. He has to survive!"

"I was really scared," muttered Mel.

"Well, I'm keeping well away from the dump, that's for sure," said Annabel.

The two girls wandered down the lane, heading for home, chatting as they went.

☆ One character might think aloud, like this:

Not for the first time, Annabel wondered about what she had done. Perhaps she shouldn't have poked her nose in. After all, her Mum was always telling her to mind her own business. But on this occasion a little bit of nosiness had paid off. She grinned to herself. Yes, it had all turned out for the best.

☆ It might be a narrator who comments:

And that was the end of the story ... well, almost the end. Annabel never did see the treasure, because only a week later the house was bulldozed to the ground and the entrance to the cellar sealed with cement. She often thought back to what had happened. In her heart she knew that she had been right to poke her nose into what was going on – but not surprisingly, it was the last time she ever trespassed.

TIME TO WRITE

Now it's time to write your story!

1 Go back to your story planner and double-check the shape of your tale. If you have had any better ideas, now is the time to make some adjustments. Keep your plan by your elbow as you write. You can add new scenes and make changes as you write, but use your plan as a guide to keep your tale on track.

2 While you are writing, you may find that sometimes your story just flows, while on other occasions you get stuck. Don't worry – this happens to every writer. If you get stuck, you could try:

★ looking at your plan to see what is meant to happen next;

★ taking the character to a new setting;

★ introducing a new character;

★ making something unexpected happen.

If you are still stuck, you might want to:

★ jot down some possible scenes and then choose one;

★ go for a walk and come back to your story later;

★ talk your story through with a friend;

★ re-read your story so far.

If none of these things help, why not leave your story for a few days and see if a new idea pops into your head?

Now – start writing! Good luck!

EDITING AND PUBLISHING

POLISHING YOUR TALE

So you've written your story – well done! What next?

Well, before you can say that your thriller is finished, you need to check it over. Look for two things. First, can the writing be improved? Second, is the writing accurate?

EDITING YOUR STORY

It can help to put your story to one side for a few weeks. When you get it out again, try to re-read it pretending that you have never seen it before. This will help you spot any places where some rewriting might improve the tale. You could read your story aloud. You may feel a bit silly doing this, but it helps you to hear how good it sounds.

You may find it helpful to ask a friend to read your story and give you feedback.

All the stories that you buy from bookshops have been checked like this by an editor. An editor reads a writer's work and suggests possible improvements and corrects any inaccuracies, before the story is published as a book.

Here are some of the things that you (or your friend) should look for.

1 Possible improvements

☆ Have you used weak words or written clumsy sentences?

☆ Do the sentences in some paragraphs need varying?

☆ Is any dialogue awkward and difficult to follow?

☆ Have you made sure that the characters sound real by showing the sort of person they are and how they feel?

☆ Are some parts of the story too rushed?

☆ Is there enough suspense?

☆ Have you used cliffhangers to make it thrilling?

☆ Do the settings help to create atmosphere?

☆ Does the story make sense?

2 Checking for accuracy

☆ Make sure your spelling, punctuation and paragraphing are all correct.

Spelling checklist

If you cannot remember a spelling, you can:

☆ Say the word slowly, listen to each sound and write them down.

☆ Write the word down, look at it and adjust the spelling till the word looks right.

☆ Think of a word you can spell that rhymes with the word you want. The spellings may be similar.

☆ Work out if there are any suffixes, prefixes or a root word that you can spell.

☆ Break the word into syllables and tackle each part at a time.

☆ Use a dictionary or spell check.

Don't avoid using a word because you cannot spell it. Do your best, and when you find out what the correct spelling is, try to remember it for next time.

Punctuation checklist

☆ Make sure that each sentence makes sense and uses a verb (unless it is a one word sentence, such as: "OK?")

☆ Don't forget exclamation marks after exclamations, such as: *Go on!*

☆ Don't forget question marks after questions, such as: *What do you want?*

☆ Don't forget to use commas to separate the items in a list – apart from before the final 'and'. For example: *Out of the box came boots, scarves, coats, hats and pyjamas!*

☆ Use a comma to separate an adverb start, such as: *Slowly, he turned.*

☆ Use a comma to separate 'ing' and 'ed' starts, such as: *Slipping, she tumbled.*

☆ Use a comma to separate a subordinate clause at the start of a sentence, such as: *Although they were cold, they stayed outside.*

coats,

scarves,

and pyjamas!

boots,

hats

☆ Use a comma when you drop a phrase or clause into a sentence, such as: *Will, whose hand was bleeding, ran downstairs.*

☆ Use speech marks to surround what is spoken (including any punctuation marks in the speech). Use a comma to lead into what is said. When a new speaker says something, start on a new line. For example:

"Hello," said Mark.

Sim replied, "Hi, how are you?"

Paragraph checklist

Long paragraphs can be hard to read.
Don't put your readers off!

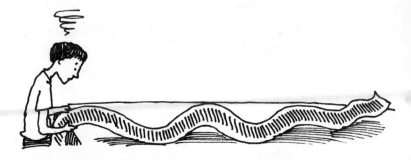

Start a new paragraph for:
☆ A change of time, for example: *Later that afternoon...*
☆ A change of place, for example:
   Back at the police station...
☆ A change of action, for
   example: *An explosion ripped
   through the silence....*
☆ A change of view, for
   example: *Mrs Savage stared
   back at Ben and wondered...*

WRITING TIP

Some writers like to check their work as they
go along. Others leave the editing till they have
finished the whole story. It's up to you when you do it.
What matters most is that you do it! Make sure you check
your work, make improvements and correct any inaccuracies
before you move on to the next stage – publishing!

PUBLISHING YOUR STORY

Well, after all that work your story is now
ready to reach your readers. You can publish
your story in lots of different ways:
- ☆ read it aloud;
- ☆ e-mail it to friends;
- ☆ turn it into a booklet
     to give to people;
- ☆ make a tape recording
     of it;
- ☆ post it on a website.

USEFUL ADDRESSES

☆ Young Writer

This is the national magazine for young writers –
and it's brilliant! It has lots of ideas and tips about
writing, in-depth interviews with well-known writers and
competitions to enter. It also publishes young writers'
stories and poems. You can visit the magazine's website
at www.youngwriter.org or phone 01544 318901.

☆ www.stonesoup.com

This website belongs to another magazine for young
writers. It provides links to loads of other great sites.
These will put you in touch with other young writers,
and give you top writing tips and opportunities to
publish your writing on the web.

GLOSSARY

adjective A word that describes somebody or something, eg *the <u>red</u> fish*.

adverb A word that adds meaning to a verb, eg *She ran <u>quickly</u>*.

alliteration A sound effect caused when a letter is repeated in words close together, eg *They <u>r</u>an <u>r</u>ound the <u>r</u>ugged <u>r</u>ocks*.

clause A group of words built around a verb, eg <u>*She was thirsty*</u>, *but <u>she didn't drink</u>*.

cliffhanger An exciting section in a story that ends abruptly, leaving a character in danger.

comma A punctuation mark (,) used to separate parts of a sentence or items in a list.

conjunction A word that links clauses or phrases within sentences, eg *Tom was silent <u>and</u> Jerry knew it was the end!*

connective A word or phrase used to link events in a story, eg <u>*The next morning*</u> *the robbers woke early*.

dialogue The words that characters speak.

dilemma A problem that characters have to solve.

dramatic tension When the story makes the reader feel anxious.

editing Re-reading a story to improve and correct it.

exclamation A sudden expression of emotion using an exclamation mark, eg *No!*

hook A clue a writer uses to tease and interest the reader.

metaphor The technique of writing about something as if it were something else, eg *Sue scampered away on mouse's paws*.

noun A word that names something or somebody, eg *The lorry stopped by the shop*.

onomatopoeia Words which sound like their meaning, eg hiss, cuckoo, buzz, crack.

paragraph A group of sentences that make up a section of writing. New paragraphs begin at a change of time, place, speaker or focus.

personification A technique in which objects are given human characteristics, eg *The wind moaned*.

phrase A group of words that work as one unit, eg *the grey-haired, old lady*.

prepositional phrase A phrase that begins with a preposition, eg *over the road, down the lane, across the street*.

science fiction Stories set in the future, in outer space or other worlds.

simile A technique in which the writer compares one thing to another, eg *The moon was like a thin smile* or *The moon was thin as a fingernail*.

speech verb A verb used to state how dialogue is spoken, eg *said* or *hissed, muttered, complained*, etc.

stylistic devices Writing techniques that add impact to writing, eg alliteration, onomatopoeia, simile, metaphor and personification.

thesaurus A type of dictionary that provides alternatives to words, eg *eat – scoff, chew, munch, gobble*, etc.

trigger An event that starts the action moving in a story.

verb A 'being' or 'doing' word, eg *She crawled down the lane. She felt petrified*.

INDEX